TONY EVANS

SPEAKS OUT ON

DIVORCE AND REMARRIAGE

TONY EVANS
SPEAKS OUT ON
DIVORCE AND
REMARRIAGE

MOODY PRESS
CHICAGO

Scripture quotations are taken from the *New American Standard Bible*®, © Copyright The Lockman Foundation 1960, 1962, 1963, 1968, 1971, 1972, 1973, 1975, 1977. Used by permission.

ISBN: 0-8024-2564-X

3 5 7 9 10 8 6 4 2

Printed in the United States of America

DIVORCE
AND
REMARRIAGE

A little girl asked, "Grandma, why is your wedding ring so big and thick?"

Her grandmother told her, "Honey, when we got married, wedding rings were made to last."

What was largely true in Grandma's day isn't so anymore. Marriage has fallen on tough times. In 1993, 2.3 million couples in America were married. In that same year, 1.2 million couples were divorced. One recent study says the chances of a marriage breaking up today are a "staggering 60 percent."

What's just as disturbing is the number of marriages where both parties remain because they feel they have to, not because they want to. It's like the unhappy spouse who said, "When I got married, I was looking for the ideal, but it became an ordeal. Now I want a new deal."

The issue of divorce and remarriage is problematic to say the least. Some people get married by a justice of the peace, but it doesn't take long before it looks like they were wed by the secretary of war. Many churches have decided to skip the issue because it is very complicated.

When it comes to divorce and remarriage, our government has decided to take the path of least resistance. So now people can get a "no-fault" divorce although I have never heard of a divorce being nobody's fault. For a few dollars and an agreement, there is no contesting the divorce. A person can get out of a marriage one day and into another one the next day.

But, as believers who claim to believe and live by God's Word, we cannot dodge this issue. We cannot skip it, run from it, or ignore it. God has spoken on marriage and divorce, and though it is not an easy subject to address, it must be dealt with.

The nature of the Christian faith, however, is not that God lowers His standards to accommodate us but that we elevate our standards to accommodate Him. We must do the adjusting, not God.

That means we are going to have to look at this subject of divorce and remarriage from God's vantage point, not simply from the vantage point of our emotions. Now, I don't want to be insensitive, because this is a human problem loaded with human feelings.

I have dealt with couples in trouble, and I know something of the pain involved. Some married people seem to be in total agony with each other. You almost wish there was some way you could open a door and help them out of their pain.

But while the emotional element of this problem is very real, we can't acquiesce to it. My purpose in this booklet is not to provide an easy exit, to put divorce on the lower shelf where it can be reached easily. How to get out of marriage is never God's mentality. Most people want to start with the "exit plan," but I want to raise marriage to a very high level because that is its nature.

I'm convinced that most people are confused about divorce because they are confused about marriage. Whenever you embark on a discussion of divorce without having predicated it on God's teaching about marriage, you have reversed the order. So let's try to get the order right.

In Malachi 2, God reveals His attitude toward divorce in light of His definition of marriage. Malachi wrote to a people who were bothered that God would not accept their worship. So, through the prophet, the Lord set out His case against the people of Israel. In the midst of this indictment we read,

> This is another thing you do: you cover the altar of the Lord with tears, with weeping and with groaning, because He no longer regards the offering or accepts it with favor from your hand. . . . The Lord has been a witness between you and the wife of your youth, against whom you have dealt treacherously, though she is your companion and your wife by *covenant*. (Malachi 2:13–14, italics added)

There it is. In that one word, *covenant,* God defines marriage for us. The reason divorce is very hard and very narrow in Scripture is that marriage is a divinely covenanted relationship. It is not just a haphazard ceremony where two people stand before a preacher, say "I do," and go home.

THREE REASONS FOR MARRIAGE

We'll look at Malachi in more detail below, but let me set the stage for our discussion by outlining the three reasons God created marriage.

The first reason for marriage is *illustration.* God wanted to illustrate His nature—one God composed of three persons. In the same way, marriage is one unit composed of three realities: husband, wife, and children. God wanted to have in history an illustration of how He is in eternity: three distinct realities composing the Godhead.

Unless you understand that marriage is designed to reflect God, you will keep it on the human level only. One of the reasons we are so quick to discount marriage is that we have kept it earthly. We have forgotten that we are illustrating the nature of God.

The second reason God created marriage is for *procreation.* Marriage is the mechanism through which children are designed to come. God does not give us children just so we can have someone who looks like us. The purpose for granting children was the replication of the image of God.

The whole idea, God said, was to "be fruitful and

multiply, and fill the earth" (Genesis 1:28). Why? Because God made us in His own image. God wants the proliferation of His image worldwide.

In other words, God wants as much of Himself in His creation as He can possibly get. So the mechanism He created to proliferate Himself was procreation via the family, where God's image would be reinforced in the life of a child in a godly environment.

Now, I realize that many married couples do not and cannot have children. Does that mean they are failing to fulfill the first two reasons for marriage?

Of course not. If God chooses to withhold children from a couple for whatever reason, that doesn't make their marriage any less valuable in His sight. They can still enjoy His blessing and reflect His holy character in their marriage.

The third reason for marriage is *self-realization*. Remember, God told Adam that he needed a helper. God was saying, "Adam, you can't do all that I want you to do by yourself. I am going to give you a helper." Eve was to work alongside Adam, to help equip and enable him to be what God wanted him to be, and in the process fulfill God's goals for her as well.

Every man who is married has been given a helper with unique gifts, talents, and resources to come alongside him and help him fulfill his role as head of the home as the family lives out God's will. Therefore, a man who does not use his wife's skills and abilities is foolish.

I have been a pastor for more than twenty-five

years, and our national ministry began in 1982. Both were built to a large degree by an unseen person, my wife, Lois, using her abilities and talents and skills. She came alongside and did a lot of the behind-the-scenes work that made the outfront things possible. Husband, not to use the resources and skills of your wife is to minimize your helper.

THE DEFINITION OF COVENANT

God had some very distinct reasons for creating marriage. And in Malachi 2:14 God calls the marriage bond itself a covenant.

What is a covenant, according to the Bible? To put it in its simplest terms, a biblical covenant is a divinely ordained contract that is predicated on relationship.

God had a covenant with Israel. The Bible calls the church a covenant. Believers gather around the table of the Lord in celebration of the "new covenant" in Christ's blood. The word *covenant* is designed to explain a unique relationship.

God always inaugurates His covenants with blood. In the Old Testament, He would kill an animal and shed its blood to seal a covenant.

When He inaugurated the new covenant, God sent Christ to earth, where He was killed and His blood was shed. There is even the shedding of blood at the inauguration of the covenant of marriage, when the bride's hymen is broken. God always inaugurates His covenants with blood.

The presence of blood shows us how serious a

covenant is. It must be bloodied in order to be legitimized. But why blood? Because it was like signing a contract. Today when we sign a contract we make it legally binding on all parties involved. A biblical covenant was always binding. It became binding and legalized when the blood was shed.

Remember those old Western movies where the white men and the Indians would draw up a treaty? They cut their hands or forearms and pressed them together to intermingle their blood because they were sealing agreement.

Now I want you to understand that a covenant is much more than a modern-day contract, because a covenant is predicated on a relationship. You can enter into a business deal and have no real relationship with the other party as long as the deal looks good. In a marriage, that's not the case, because marriage is a covenant. It's based on relationship.

If you want to be part of the family of God, you must enter into a relationship with Jesus Christ. A covenant is more than a contract, even though covenants have contractual elements. When you enter into a covenant, you commit yourself to a relationship. That's what you do when you get married.

Of course, that is not being taught much today, so people don't really know what they are doing when they marry. They know it's kind of serious somehow, but it's not that serious. Well, marriage is very serious to God, according to Malachi 2:14. It is His covenant.

This whole concept is so important that I want to

look at five truths about covenants before we talk about the specific issues involved in divorce and remarriage. Remember, until we understand God's standards and ideal for marriage, we won't know how to deal with the issue of divorce.

COVENANTS ARE ESTABLISHED BY GOD

First of all, all legitimate covenants in Scripture are established by God. They're His covenants.

Marriage is not *your* covenant. It's God's covenant. You must understand this. Yes, you are a participant in it, but it is God's covenant, and, as such, He makes the rules.

Notice once again that Malachi 2:14 says concerning the marriages of the Israelites, "the Lord has been a witness between you and the wife of your youth." That word *witness* means "legal accuser," like a witness taking the stand. God is in the heavenly court testifying against the people because they were divorcing their wives and breaking His covenant.

Remember, God's covenants are contractual. They are always legalized, but they are legalized in heaven before they are recognized on earth. So God was a witness against the Israelites when it came to their violation of the marriage covenant.

Now, most people respect the fact that God has something to do with the covenant of marriage. That's why they get married in church. When a minister marries you, he asks you if you promise to do this, that, and the other "for as long as you both shall live, so help you God."

Why does the minister bring in God's name? Because he understands that a covenant is established by God. That's why in the Bible, if you had a legitimate ground for a divorce, you had to get what was called a "certificate of divorce." You could not just go out and get divorced. It had to be legally recognized.

Observe God's guidelines if you want God's blessings.

This is very important, because if a covenant is established by God, *it can only be ended by God*. Now, that is not what people want to hear. They want God to approve the wedding, but they don't want Him involved in the divorce. They want God's blessing on the marriage, but they don't care what He thinks about the divorce.

Sorry, it doesn't work that way. This is why, if you get a divorce that is not permitted under the conditions we will talk about later, when you marry somebody else God says you commit adultery. The reason you commit adultery is that, in God's eyes, you are not free from your first covenant. God says marriage is His covenant, and He is the only one who can release you from it.

Most people don't have that view. They view their

marriage as theirs alone. "God, You were welcome at the altar. But now that we are going on the honeymoon, You can stay at church."

So, marriage is a covenant established by God. That's why Jesus said, "What therefore God has joined together, let no man separate" (Matthew 19:6). When you go before the judge downtown, you give him the power to overrule God—and God will not be overruled.

God is saying, "This is My covenant and My institution, so you must function under My guidelines if you want My blessings." You must understand this fundamental truth. Otherwise, if you just rush in and get married, then you are going to mess up.

And by the way, this is not just for Christians. God recognizes all marriages, even those between two non-Christians, because marriage is a divine institution given to the human race (Matthew 19:4–6). This is why John the Baptist could condemn Herod Antipas for his adultery (Matthew 14:1–4). God even recognized the marriage of a pagan ruler such as Herod.

COVENANTS FUNCTION
UNDER A CHAIN OF COMMAND

A second truth about covenants is that all covenants function under divine authority. Since covenants are established by God, they must function under a divinely prescribed chain of command.

In Malachi 2, God says He condemned the Israelite men because they were discarding their legitimate wives. Among their many other spiritual problems, these people did not understand a fundamental principle in Scripture: the principle of representation.

If you are a Christian, the reason you are not going to hell is that you have changed representatives. You are no longer in Adam. You are in Christ. He is your new representative. In 1 Corinthians 11:3, Paul says that Christ is under God, every Christian man is under Christ, and the woman is under the man. In Ephesians 6:1, Paul says children are under their parents. Everybody is linked in God's chain of command.

This explains something very important: the methodology of Satan in the Garden of Eden. Notice that Satan never bothered Adam when he was single. He had to get married before the devil showed up.

Why didn't Satan tempt Adam while he was in the Garden by himself? Satan understood the principle of representation and what would happen if this chain got kinked up.

So who did the serpent approach, the head of the house? Did he go to Adam? No. He conversed with Eve. What Satan did was produce a break in the chain. Eve became the leader, Adam the follower. Their roles were reversed. And Satan was in charge of both of them.

That's why, Christian man, if Satan can make you a passive husband and father and turn your wife into a fully liberated woman so that she doesn't need you and wants to operate independently of you, then he switches your roles. And if he switches your roles, he owns you.

Two major reasons for divorce today are the failure

of men to take seriously their roles as lovers and leaders in the home, and the failure of wives and mothers to prioritize family over career.

Now don't misunderstand me. There's nothing wrong with a woman having a job and striving to do her best in her career. But her career is always to be secondary to the priority of the home (Proverbs 31:10–31; 1 Timothy 5:13–14; Titus 2:3–5).

Christian woman, if your job makes being a wife and mother secondary in your life, you are inviting Satan into your home. It is better to have less with your priorities in place than to have more without them.

This principle of authority says that, as we function under God, then we get the blessing, because the blessing flows through the chain.

COVENANTS HAVE RULES

Third, all covenants have rules, that is, specific guidelines that govern how they are to operate. Just as anyone living in my house must adjust to my rules, anyone living in God's house must adjust to His rules. You cannot enter God's covenant and make up your own rules as you go along. Many people want to live out their own rules in God's marriage covenant, but they do so at their own risk.

God has clearly prescribed the role that each party in the marriage covenant is to have. A husband is to lead and love his wife; he is to sacrifice whatever is necessary to help her develop into all God wants her to be.

A wife, on the other hand, is to reverence her husband, holding him in high esteem and rendering verbal and visible recognition of his God-ordained position as head. This involves a submission that uses all of her gifts, skills, and abilities under the leadership of her husband to promote God's agenda for the home. Only when husbands and wives fulfill their God-ordained roles can they expect to experience God's blessing and power in the covenant of marriage.

God's complaint against the Israelites in Malachi's day is the same complaint He has against us today: They were not abiding by His rules for marriage.

COVENANTS HAVE SANCTIONS

A fourth truth about God's covenants is that they carry sanctions. These are the blessings or cursings that attach to the covenant and that kick in depending on our obedience or disobedience.

"Since you are not following My rules," God was saying in Malachi, "I will not accept your offerings." To put it another way, if you don't follow God's rules, you suffer the consequences. There is a built-in cause/relationship.

You say that is Old Testament. No, it's New Testament too: "You husbands . . . , live with your wives in an understanding way, as with a weaker vessel . . . so that your prayers may not be hindered" (1 Peter 3:7). Here's the same principle. When you forsake God's rules, you lose God's blessing.

If we as husbands and wives are not doing what we know He wants us to do, then we shouldn't be surprised if the hand of God is not felt in our homes.

To see an example of the sanctions of a covenant spelled out very clearly, all you have to do is read Deuteronomy 28, where the rules of God's covenant with Israel are specified with accompanying cursings and blessings. Sanctions say, if you do this, this is what will happen. If you do that, that is what will happen. There is no question about the sanctions. You choose whether you are going to obey.

How does this apply to marriage? You have to get a marriage license before you can get married. There are also witnesses at the wedding who sign the marriage license, verifying that this wedding did in fact take place and that the bride and groom made certain promises to each other and to God.

There are also many other witnesses in the audience, and of course the minister is a witness. Now we don't bother with this these days, but these witnesses could be called forth in court to give testimony that a husband and wife did indeed enter into the covenant of marriage. Then, if one or both parties had broken the covenant, the sanctions of that covenant could be invoked by the judge.

Like I said, we don't take marriage seriously enough to go to that much trouble. But God takes His covenants very seriously. And His sanctions include death. When you break God's covenant, you die. Always.

What do I mean by that? God said to Adam and Eve concerning the forbidden tree, "In the day that you eat from it you shall surely die" (Genesis 2:17). Adam and Eve did not die for hundreds of years. But God had said they would die the very day they ate from the forbidden tree.

I submit to you that they did die that day. In what way? Well, that same day, our first parents were excommunicated from the Garden of Eden. In other words, they were removed from fellowship with God.

It's clear that the biblical meaning of death is separation, not just cessation of physical life. When you break God's covenant, you are immediately separated from His presence. That doesn't mean you fall down and stop breathing. It means that you are cut off from fellowship with God.

COVENANTS HAVE CONSEQUENCES

Fifth and finally, covenants have consequences that go beyond the immediate parties involved. Your decision about marriage not only affects you, it affects your offspring. All you have to do is look at our society to see that.

People's decisions to break their marriage covenants are being reflected in their offspring—to "the third and fourth generations" (Exodus 20:5). This thing will keep on spinning and spinning out of control, because, when you break a covenant, the impact of that may transfer through you to the generations after you. One reason I want to stay married is not simply related to me, but for the generations that will come after me.

So what I am saying is that before we can talk about divorce, we need to talk about marriage. Divorce does not just end a marriage, it could involve the breaking of a covenant, and you don't want to do that lightly.

When you got married, you made a pledge. You promised to love and cherish and honor your partner "till death do us part." In other words, the one thing that can end this relationship is death. With this understanding of marriage, it is little wonder that God hates divorce (Malachi 2:16).

JESUS ON MARRIAGE AND DIVORCE

Let's go to Matthew 19, where the Pharisees sought to trick Jesus by asking Him what they thought was a tough question about divorce. Matthew says they were "testing Him" (v. 3), meaning they weren't serious about their question. They just wanted to catch Jesus between the proverbial rock and a hard place.

So they asked Him, "Is it lawful for a man to divorce his wife for any cause at all?" (v. 3). Or, to put it in modern-day vernacular, can you get a no-fault divorce for any reason you want?

In Jesus' day, much like today, there were two schools of thought in the religious community regarding divorce. The conservative Jews and their rabbis held that a person could not get divorced for any reason at all. The liberal Jews and their rabbis held that a person could get divorced for almost any reason.

So Jesus was being asked to decide this Jewish controversy. Of course, He knew what their motive was, and He wasn't about to fall into their trap. He began by asking them, "Have you not read?" (v. 4). In other words, "Don't you have a Bible?" What Jesus was saying is that this issue should not be left up to discussion, debate, or personal viewpoints.

See, when it comes to divorce, everybody has an opinion. If you are having marital difficulties, you can always find somebody who is going to make you comfortable about your position.

But Jesus was not interested in popular opinion. He didn't wet His finger and stick it in the air to see which way the wind was blowing. He took the Pharisees right back to Scripture, to the very beginning in Genesis 1–2.

The great tragedy about marriage and divorce is that we listen to everybody else, but we do not read what God has said about it. We must read His Word on this critical subject, because marriage is God's idea. We're talking about a divine relationship, a divinely authored and ordained institution.

Marriage was designed to be permanent.

So the issue isn't what people say, but what God says. When God created Adam and Eve and performed the first marriage, divorce was not part of the formula. It was never God's intention that there would be even one case of divorce. God said, "I hate divorce" (Malachi 2:16). It is outside of His intention and ideal.

That's why Jesus chided the Pharisees for not going

back to the Scripture to see what God said about marriage and, particularly, divorce. In Matthew 19:4-5 He rehearsed that first marriage ceremony for the Pharisees, then added a word of His own in verse 6: "They are no longer two, but one flesh. What therefore God has joined together, let no man separate."

So Jesus does the same thing we have just done when confronted with the question of divorce. He says that before we can talk about divorce, we need to talk about God's original will and plan for marriage. When God orchestrates a marriage, He intends it to be a one-flesh commitment for life.

Now the reason this is so is that it takes a lifetime to get marriage right. So many people say, "Well, I didn't know this is what I was getting into."

Of course you didn't know. You weren't married yet. And when you did get married, you did not marry just your mate. You married his or her family, as well as the family history. You married parts of the person's mama, parts of his or her daddy, and parts of the grandparents. You married a long line of traits, experiences, and attitudes, but you didn't realize that because your potential mate covered all that up while you were dating.

She did not let you see that you were marrying the nagging habits she learned from her mama. He did not tell you that you were marrying the insensitivity he accumulated from his father. The reason God says marriage is one flesh for life is that when you get married you pick up all of that along with your new spouse, and it takes a lifetime to get a marriage right.

So Jesus reminded the Pharisees that marriage was designed to be a permanent relationship. It is God's institution. He made the people for marriage. He came up with the idea of marriage, and He gave us the ideal for marriage, two becoming one flesh. It was all God's agenda.

Therefore, as we saw above in verse 6, Jesus said that, since God does the joining, no man has the right to do the separating. Let me give you the "Evans paraphrase" of verse 6: "What God has joined together, only God can separate." The contrast here is between human beings and God.

The last time I checked, the judge downtown at the courthouse was just a person. Whenever you let a human judge—or any human authority—overrule God, you have placed God under man. But Jesus says it is God who has joined these two people together, and no human has the right to separate them.

I know some people will say they don't believe God brought them together. But I say they do. That's why they got married in church by a preacher who used the Bible. That is why they said "I do" when the preacher asked them if they vowed to stay married to this person until death. They just changed their minds after they found out all they got into when they got married.

Now, here is where we start getting to the issue of divorce. It was obvious even in the days of Moses that God's ideal for marriage was not always being realized because of human sin. Some allowance had to be made, but it needed to be made on God's terms, not man's. Although man should not be able to overrule God's covenant of marriage, God can overrule His own covenant in certain extreme cases.

Here is an important distinction that many people don't grasp. Look at the exchange between Jesus and the Pharisees in verses 7–8 of Matthew 19. Remember, the question on the floor is whether a man can divorce his wife for any cause at all:

> They said to Him, "Why then did Moses command to give her a certificate and divorce her?" He said to them, "Because of your hardness of heart Moses permitted you to divorce your wives; but from the beginning it has not been this way."

Notice the very different words that the Pharisees and Jesus use to describe divorce. They called it a command, implying that it was something they had to do, something Moses was making them do. But Jesus set them straight right away by saying that it was a permission, a concession because of sin, not a command.

God never commands divorce. But because of sin, God sometimes allows divorce. That's a fundamental distinction. God never tells you that you have to get a divorce. But there are certain situations in which God will permit people the option of getting a divorce because of sin.

There were several reasons for the certificate of divorce mentioned here. It was a document showing that the divorce had been granted legally. These are still issued today—although much too easily. But the idea is that if you got married legally, you had to get divorced legally.

The divorce certificate also provided a way to protect the innocent from the ravages of sin. Protection became an important factor here. Even in the Garden, when God divorced himself from Adam and Eve and removed them, it was to protect His holiness and prevent them from getting to the tree of life in their sinful condition.

The certificate of divorce was the only way women in biblical times could be protected. Women could easily be abused without this certificate, because it made certain provisions for them. Otherwise, if a man could just throw his wife out of the house because he wanted to, she and perhaps even the children might be put out on the streets. If divorce were legally established, then it had to be obtained legally.

The Pharisees tried to trick Jesus with a little word switch here, but of course it didn't work. He reminded them that God only permitted divorce. He did not command it under Moses, and He does not command it today.

So the question becomes under what circumstances God permits divorce. Jesus addresses that in verse 9: "And I say to you, whoever divorces his wife, except for immorality, and marries another [woman] commits adultery." A permissible basis for divorce is immorality by one of the parties in a marriage.

Now notice. Jesus says that if you get divorced for an illegitimate reason, then go out and marry someone else, you commit adultery. Why? Because in God's mind, you are still married to the person you thought you divorced.

But someone may say, "I went downtown and stood before the judge, and he granted me a divorce. I've got the papers to show it's all legal. The judge said so." Wrong judge. Jesus says, "Don't let men put asunder what God has joined together."

What Jesus says is that it's not enough to go before the judge downtown and have him tell you that you are divorced and free to go out and remarry if the Judge uptown, God Himself, doesn't say you are divorced.

How do you know if a possible divorce is biblically permissible? As we'll see later, God has given the church authority to rule in cases like this. No believer should head downtown to divorce court until he or she has brought his or her case to the church for a determination of the facts and a ruling. Now, if the church finds no grounds for divorce, the person might still choose to go ahead and get a divorce downtown. But one does so at one's own spiritual peril.

That's because, as far as God is concerned, a person who divorces with no legitimate grounds is still married to his or her first partner. So, if that person remarries on the word of the judge downtown and not on the Word of the Judge uptown, he or she now has two living mates. And the more illegitimate divorces and remarriages, the greater the number of living mates left behind.

IMMORALITY AND DIVORCE

Since Jesus specifically cited immorality as legitimate grounds for divorce—again, meaning that divorce is permissible, not required—we need to find out what the Bible means by the term *immorality*.

This word was used for a whole host of illicit acts and relationships. It was not just one type of thing. Look at what Moses says in Leviticus 18:3: "You shall not do what is done in the land of Egypt where you lived, nor are you to do what is done in the land of Canaan where I am bringing you; you shall not walk in their statutes."

Moses is saying, "I don't care what they did in Egypt. This is not Egypt. You are God's people living under His covenant, which means you operate under different rules."

We could say today, "It doesn't matter what they say downtown. It doesn't matter what allowances they make at the courthouse and how quick you can get a divorce downtown. This is not downtown. This is the church, the covenant people of God."

Moses went on in Leviticus 18 to enumerate a whole list of sexual sins and abominations that were forbidden to God's people, including incest (vv. 6–16), adultery (v. 20), homosexuality (v. 22), and bestiality (v. 23).

Then he summarized in verse 29 by saying, "Whoever does any of these abominations, those persons who do so shall be cut off from among their people," which automatically meant that their marriages would have been ended. Thus, a capital crime was also a divorceable crime if the guilty party was not executed.

That is, sexual immorality in its various forms was a capital crime in the Old Testament. This was still considered to be true in Jesus' day, as we know from the story of the woman caught in adultery (John 8:1–11). So immorality was a very serious offense.

But why did Jesus mention immorality as permissible grounds for divorce? Because according to 1 Corinthians 6:15–16, when you have sexual intercourse with another person you create an illegitimate covenant:

> Do you not know that your bodies are members of Christ? Shall I then take away the members of Christ and make them members of a harlot? May it never be! Or do you not know that the one who joins himself to a harlot is one body with her? For He says, "The two will become one flesh."

Notice that Paul uses the language of marriage in verse 16 to describe what happens when a man goes out and spends one night with a prostitute, or when a woman has an affair. Now, if these people are already married, their immorality has created a rival covenant to their marriage covenant.

If the person who does this is unrepentant, and especially if he or she persists in having illicit affairs, that gives the offended party in their marriage grounds for divorce.

Sometimes, it may be wise to divorce even if the offender is repentant. For example, suppose a husband enters into an immoral relationship. Afterward he is repentant, but finds out that he has AIDS. Now, his wife has a serious problem, even though she may forgive him for his sin. She would be risking her life to live with him again as husband and wife.

That's a really tough one, but it's one example of a time that divorce based on immorality might be wise, even if the offending party is repentant. Let me say again, though, that even in extreme cases like this, divorce is not required. It is not in God's original design for marriage. It is only a concession because of sin.

So the issue of sex is really theological, not biological. It has to do with establishing a covenant. Look at what Jesus says in Matthew 5:31–32:

> It was said, "Whoever divorces his wife, let him give her a certificate of dismissal;" but I say to you that every one who divorces his wife, except for the cause of unchastity, makes her commit adultery; and whoever marries a divorced woman commits adultery.

Here we have what is called a mess. A man divorces his wife (although the same truth applies the other way) for some reason we'll call "irreconcilable differences," the catch-all phrase for quick divorces today, although it's unheard of in the Bible.

This man then marries someone else, but according to Matthew 19 he has just committed adultery because in God's eyes he is still married to his first wife.

But now it gets messy. The wife who is divorced marries another man, so she commits adultery. But in Matthew 5, she is not blamed. The husband is blamed for putting her in that situation. So he causes his ex-wife to commit adultery. But the other man and woman who marry these two former marriage partners are committing adultery, because they are marrying people who are still married to someone else in God's sight.

You may need a minute to sort that one out. The bottom line is that all four parties in this scenario are involved in adultery. As I said, it's a mess.

And that's exactly what we have today—a mess—because people are breaking their marriage covenant with God apart from His permission. This is serious business. Jesus says you can't just divorce for any reason.

PAUL ON MARRIAGE AND DIVORCE

In 1 Corinthians 7, the apostle Paul adds to what Jesus Christ says about marriage and divorce. And he starts the same way Jesus did, with marriage as it should be, before he moves to the problems. Of course, what Paul writes is the authoritative Word of God, so let's look at verses 3–5, where he discusses the issue of marital intimacy:

> Let the husband fulfill his duty to his wife, and likewise also the wife to her husband. The wife does not have authority over her own body, but the husband does; and likewise also the husband does not have authority over

his own body, but the wife does. Stop depriving one another, except by agreement for a time that you may devote yourselves to prayer, and come together again lest Satan tempt you because of your lack of self-control.

Regular sexual intimacy is the ideal for a married couple. The only exception is for special times where the partners agree to abstain from sex so they can commit themselves to intense prayer. Even these times, Paul says, should be limited.

Now, anyone who's married knows you can't be intimate on a regular basis if you and your mate are not getting along, if you are driving each other crazy. But incompatibility is not grounds for divorce:

> But to the married I give instructions, not I, but the Lord, that the wife should not leave her husband (but if she does leave, let her remain unmarried, or else be reconciled to her husband), and that the husband should not send his wife away. (vv. 10–11)

If there are irreconcilable differences in a marriage and a separation occurs, the partners must not marry another. Why? Because they are still married to each other.

Notice, however, that the goal is to reconcile with each other, not to turn the separation into a permanent one through a divorce designed to free up the person to marry someone else. Note also that in Paul's example, the mate of the woman who leaves is still called her husband.

But if a partner goes ahead and divorces for irreconcilable differences, the only way God does not call that person an adulteress or an adulterer is if he or she stays unmarried. God still recognizes the original covenant. Irreconcilable differences may lead to a separation, but, in that case, the only options given by God are to remain unmarried or be reconciled.

But in cases of abandonment (vv. 12–15), Paul does give another option. Once again, Paul begins with the best-case scenario, when one partner is an unbeliever. If the unbeliever is willing to stay in the marriage, let him or her stay because then the Christian partner becomes an evangelist.

If this is your situation, your job is to win your mate to the Savior. There are plenty of illustrations of godly women in particular who have led their husbands to Christ over time.

But if the unbelieving partner leaves, the believer is "not under bondage in such cases" (v. 15), which I take to mean that the believer is free. Abandonment can take a number of forms. It may be physically leaving the home, or it may be one of the partners forsaking his or her role in the relationship.

Then, the Bible says the believer does not have to go to extreme measures to keep the marriage together. So we have two legitimate grounds for divorce: immorality and abandonment by a non-Christian partner.

Now, this solves some of our problems, but not all of them. What about a believer who abandons his responsibility to his family, even if he doesn't pack up and leave?

Perhaps he is on drugs, or he has a gambling habit and the wife can't buy milk for the kids because he is gambling all the money away. Or he refuses to work and support his family. Or he's physically abusing his wife and children. What then?

Well, let me start by going back to Romans 7, where we read that a woman is bound to her husband as long as he lives, but if he dies, she is free to marry another. When a mate dies, a new marriage can be inaugurated.

This is important, because I believe that this provision includes more than physical death. We've already talked about the fact that in the Bible spiritual death is as real as physical death. Remember, the Bible says that Adam and Eve did die the day they ate the forbidden fruit, because they were put out of the Garden and cut off from fellowship with God. They were dead spiritually.

Let me show you how this sanction applies to marriage. The Bible teaches that death breaks the covenant of marriage. Look at Romans 7:1–3:

> Do you not know, brethren (for I am speaking to those who know the law), that the law has jurisdiction over a person as long as he lives? For the married woman is bound by law to her husband while he is living; but if her husband dies, she is released from the law concerning the husband. So then if, while her husband is living, she is joined to another man, she shall be called an adulteress; but if her husband dies, she is free from the law, so that she is not an adulteress, though she is joined to another man.

This principle helps us to understand the issue of divorce, because, biblically speaking, divorce always revolves around one question: Is the person you are thinking about divorcing alive or dead? It all boils down to that. If your mate is still alive, then of course you are still married. If your mate is dead, then you are free to marry another person.

Now, at this point you are probably thinking I have just stated something that is blatantly obvious. If a spouse dies, it's clear that the marriage is over and the surviving spouse is free to remarry.

But I'm going to show you that this principle also holds true in the spiritual as well as in the physical realm. We know from Scripture that spiritual death is as real as physical death. Therefore, just as when a husband or wife dies physically his or her mate can be released from the marriage, so can the mate of a person who dies spiritually be released from the marriage.

As I said above, then, death is the only legitimate grounds for divorce. We will talk later about what constitutes spiritual death and what can kill a marriage. As I said above, there is more than one meaning for death in the Bible. In the case of physical death, it is obvious that the marriage has ended and the surviving partner is then free to remarry. Everyone agrees with that.

But spiritual death can also destroy a marriage. So the questions are, What constitutes spiritual death, and how does spiritual death kill a marriage?

This principle operates in Paul's discussion in Romans 7 for three reasons. First, at the end of Romans chapter 6 we find the statement that "the wages of sin is death." Sin brings spiritual as well as physical death. Second, Paul's reference to the Law in Romans 7 refers to the old covenant, so when a man dies he dies to a covenant relationship. Third, Paul specifically says in verse 4 that spiritual death to one covenant allows for remarriage to another covenant. Paul's reference to death is clearly both physical and spiritual.

So when a person breaks covenant with God and is removed from fellowship with Him, the Bible calls that person dead. Now look at 1 Corinthians 5, the case of the man who was having an affair with his step-mother.

These two were living in open sin, and the church did nothing about it. In verse 5 Paul says he delivered this man over to Satan "for the destruction of his flesh, that his spirit may be saved in the day of the Lord Jesus." This man was excommunicated from the church and transferred to the realm of death, the realm of Satan. As far as God was concerned, he was dead until he repented.

So once again immorality is dealt with head-on. But according to verse 11, a believer could also be removed from the fellowship of the church for a number of other reasons, including being a reviler or a swindler or covetous or a drunkard.

And this person was to be considered spiritually dead unless he repented. This is why Jesus says in Matthew 18:17 that, if a believer won't listen to the church, he is to be treated as a "Gentile and tax collector" —as a sinner, in other words.

Sinners are spiritually dead, right? So even if this person is a Christian, you treat him as though he were a sinner with the sentence of death over him. What about his marriage if he is married? Well, if he is dead, then his marriage is dead, and his wife is free under the provisions of Romans 7 and 1 Corinthians 7:39.

Now don't misunderstand me or run ahead of me here. Let me tell you what I am and am not saying. I am saying that spiritual death, or what I call covenantal death in relation to marriage, is a broader category than just sexual immorality or desertion.

But I am *not* saying that this throws the doors wide open to divorce or gives someone a new way out he or she hadn't thought of before. Why? First, because covenantal death still doesn't alter God's ideal for marriage. And second, even in a case where a spouse may seek permission for divorce based on the covenantal death of the other partner, the church still needs to investigate the case thoroughly and see if the charge is valid. Granting permission for divorce is still the most extreme step to take.

For example, if a wife comes to the church and says her husband refuses to work and support the family, that charge has to be looked at carefully. We're not talking about a case of his not working for a week, or his being laid off and laboring unsuccessfully to find new employment.

But if he says, "I have no intention of working and supporting my wife and family, and I never will, no matter what you say or the church says"—in that extreme case, the church has the authority to declare the husband covenantally dead and to give the wife permission for divorce.

This is the problem-solving approach to dealing with people who aren't immoral but who are living in rebellion and have abandoned or are abusing their mates. Is the Bible saying to a wife, "He hasn't slept with anybody else, so stay there and get beaten, abused, or neglected for the rest of your life"?

No, but again the Bible never says you have to get a divorce. God does not command divorce. He just permits it, and He recognizes that believers can get to the point that they are functioning at a lower level in their marriage relationships than even unbelievers (1 Timothy 5:8).

Let me summarize the three realms where divorce is permissible, each involving some level of spiritual death:

1. When a mate enters into an illegitimate covenant by committing immorality with another person.
2. When a Christian is abandoned by a non-Christian.
3. When a Christian is living in the realm of death and it has been officially recognized by the church, so that this person's mate is declared eligible for a certificate of divorce.

In cases like these the job of the church, as we will see, is to serve as God's court. Before going downtown to get a piece of paper, believers are to submit their cases to the church. If the case is extreme enough to make divorce permissible, the church can issue a certificate of divorce that is recognized by God based on recognition by the church. Then the person has the freedom to make the divorce legal downtown.

When a person dies, you don't need a lay opinion, you need a coroner's opinion. You can't just say a person looked like he was dead. There must be an official recognition of death. God's coroner is the church. In the case of a marriage, where there is spiritual death there is freedom to divorce—even though this freedom does not have to be taken, especially if there is sincere repentance.

Now, what does all this mean? Once you have a certificate of divorce, you have the right to remarry. Any legitimate grounds for divorce is automatically an allowance for remarriage. But God takes marriage seriously, and you can't dissolve a relationship until a death occurs, whether physical death or spiritual death through adultery, abandonment, or excommunication from the church.

These areas are broad enough to cover the issue. There is probably not a case that doesn't fit under one of these headings.

GOD'S COURT

You say, "Where does God tell the church to serve as a court for possible divorce cases?"

Well, we're going to go there right now. In fact, I

want to begin with a passage we've already considered, 1 Corinthians 5—except that now, we need to flow over into chapter 6, because the opening verses of chapter 6 belong to the issue Paul is discussing. Remember, the Bible's chapter divisions are a later addition, so chapter 6 is really the continuation of chapter 5.

We saw that 1 Corinthians 5 deals with removing a sinning member from the fellowship of the church. Verse 11 says not to associate with "any so-called brother if he should be an immoral person, or covetous, or an idolater, or a reviler, or a drunkard, or a swindler— not even to eat with such a one."

Therefore, relational fellowship can be broken for any number of reasons. The church's job in these cases is to judge those within its ranks (v. 12). In chapter 6, Paul explains how this process of judgment is to be carried out. He begins with a question: "Does any one of you, when he has a case against his neighbor, dare to go to law before the unrighteous, and not before the saints?" (v. 1).

"How dare you," Paul says, "go to the unrighteous to decide matters that concern the righteous." This is strong language, implying that the idea of going to a civil court controlled by men who do not know God to render a judgment between people who know God is unthinkable.

Paul is saying to the saints, "You don't know who you are" (see v. 2). Well, who are we? We are those who are going to judge the world with Christ when He "will sit on His glorious throne" (Matthew 19:28). We will also judge fallen angels (1 Corinthians 6:3).

Judgment is a part of our role as God's people. If we are going to judge on that level, Paul says, certainly we can serve as a small claims court, including rendering judgment on cases of potential divorce.

Notice that Paul confers on the church a legal status, making it a legal entity. Not legal in terms of the government, but legal in terms of the kingdom. Kingdom decisions are to be rendered by kingdom people, those who obligate themselves to kingdom rule. Therefore, kingdom decisions about kingdom people must be made by the kingdom's court.

Jesus is not telling us to avoid judging others.

Why? Because only the kingdom's court has the divine perspective and can render decisions based on the King's standards. That's why the Bible calls the church a court.

Now, most churches run from this because it is hard work. But the church was never intended to be a building where you go for two hours of services once a week. It was intended to be the expression of the kingdom, an extension of the King's rule.

Some people also try to get around our duty to judge by pointing to Matthew 7:1, where Jesus said,

"Do not judge lest you be judged yourselves."

Jesus said that all right, but the problem comes when you stop there and close your Bible. Verse 2 explains what Jesus is talking about. He is not saying don't ever judge anyone. He is urging us to be careful when we judge, because the same judgment we use against another person will be the judgment God uses against us. The idea is to think twice before you make a judgment.

In other words, Jesus is saying we need to judge other people and situations carefully. We have just seen that Christians are commanded to judge. As people with access to the truth of God, we ought to be the best qualified to judge correctly.

The problem Jesus was dealing with was hypocritical judgment, people who need to deal with things in their own lives but who are trying to judge others. That's why the church needs to be sure that, when it sits to judge God's people, it does so with a clean heart and with God's perspective.

Jesus is not telling us to avoid judging others. He is saying to be careful how and when you judge. In fact, when Jesus prayed, "Thy will be done, on earth as it is in heaven" (Matthew 6:10), He was saying that there is a realm in which God's will is to be carried out in history. It is called His kingdom, and it is run by His church. So, like it or not, judgment is a part of our ministry as the people of God.

When it comes to "matters of this life," Paul says that the church should not be appointing judges who have no jurisdiction in the family of God. So when a couple decides they want a divorce, they shouldn't take their case to the unrighteous, who have no kingdom view of marriage, who don't understand that God is the author of marriage, and who simply grant a no-fault divorce.

Now, Paul is not saying civil courts are wrong. You must have civil government, because the righteous aren't the only ones who live here. But when it comes to matters of the kingdom, things like legal disputes between believers and divorce cases, they are to be decided within the kingdom. Ideally, these decisions would be confirmed by the government—although in the matter of divorce we know that divorce isn't likely to become harder to obtain.

This matter of judgment is so important to the church's agenda that Paul says in 1 Corinthians 6:5 that the Corinthians should be ashamed that they couldn't get their act together here. He chides them for not using the spiritual wisdom God had given them.

In fact, Paul goes on to say, beginning in verse 7, that, if two believers have to go to a secular law court to settle a matter, they have already lost for two reasons. First, because they have destroyed their testimony. Second, because God is against the process. So the church is to act as God's judging agency.

OLD TESTAMENT EXAMPLES

In the Old Testament, God also established His courts and granted them real authority. In Deuteronomy 17:8–10, Moses instructed the people of Israel:

If any case is too difficult for you to decide, between one kind of homicide or another, between one kind of lawsuit or another, and between one kind of assault or another, being cases of dispute in your courts, then you shall arise and go up to the place which the Lord your God chooses. So you shall come to the Levitical priest or the judge who is in office in those days, and you shall inquire of them and they will declare to you the verdict in the case. And you shall do according to the terms of the verdict which they declare to you from that place which the Lord chooses; and you shall be careful to observe according to all that they teach you.

Read on through verse 12 and you'll see that the verdict was final! The point is that God's court system was to be taken seriously, because it had God's authority and His power behind it.

In Numbers 5:11–31 we read about the steps that were to be taken by the priest to determine if a wife had been unfaithful to her husband. Although the details of this process sound strange to our modern ears, don't miss the significance of what's going on here. The priest acted as God's judge, and God Himself was directly involved in the process (v. 16) so that the truth was known and real justice was rendered.

This was called the "law of jealousy" (v. 29), but it was not just a petty jealousy thing. It was a serious accusation and a serious trial. Notice in verse 22 that the woman said, "Amen. Amen" to the process.

Amen means "So be it. I agree with what is being said or done." The woman was agreeing to accept the result of the Lord's judgment, whether blessing or cursing. She was saying that she understood what would come upon her as a result of the trial, and she was willing to accept God's verdict.

Obviously, this was a very serious statement for the woman to make. You get the idea, I think. God's Old Testament courts were powerful entities with His authority not only to render decisions, but to execute them.

Now Paul says in 1 Corinthians 10:11 that these things in the Old Testament were written for our example as believers today. In other words, we can use the Old Testament not for its regulations, but for its revelation. The principle of God's people rendering His judgments still applies, even though the specifics of how that's carried out may not be the same today.

God still wants His people to render judgment on His behalf when there is a dispute. These kinds of cases come up constantly in the church, whether it is two Christian business people who can't agree or a dispute concerning a contract or transaction made between two Christians.

THE PROCESS OF JUDGING

The issue is, do you sue your brother or sister in secular court? Do you haul the person downtown, or do you take the issue to the church? Well, the Bible is clear. You take it to the church. Jesus Himself explained the process in Matthew 18:15–17. Let's talk about it as it applies to the issue of divorce:

If your brother sins, go and reprove him in private; if he listens to you, you have won your brother. But if he does not listen to you, take one or two more with you, so that by the mouth of two or three witnesses every fact may be confirmed. And if he refuses to listen to them, tell it to the church; and if he refuses to listen even to the church, let him be to you as a Gentile and a tax gatherer.

The first thing you do with a dispute is attempt to handle it personally. If a fellow believer or your mate has hurt you, the first thing you do is try to fix it privately. You never carry a problem beyond the circle of those who need to know about it.

Notice how Jesus widens the circle when it becomes appropriate. If the other party does not listen to you, is not open to correction, is not repentant, then other witnesses can be brought in.

The involvement of witnesses meant that there was a legality attached to the process now. It became official. In the case of a married couple, the offended party is trying to fix this marriage, but the other partner won't have it. It's not a matter of one mate's word against the other's, because there are witnesses to corroborate the accusation.

But if that steps fails, then the issue is to be brought before the church body. Why? Because the church is this couple's extended family. It's the environment where God's decisions are rendered.

The church's leaders should be capable of judging whether the offense is genuine and whether the possibility of forgiveness and reconciliation exists in this marriage. If not, the church should be ready to render a judgment as to whether the offended mate has grounds for divorce. And, of course, the couple should be willing to submit to the church's decision.

But if the offender will not listen to the church, if he is unrepentant, then Jesus says he is to be excommunicated from the fellowship and treated as a spiritually dead person, an unbeliever. That's exactly what Paul says too.

To make His point, Jesus chose the two groups of people who were ostracized by the Jewish community of His day. Tax collectors were Jews who worked for Rome. They were rejected by the broader Jewish community because of their occupation. And no good Jew would have any fellowship with a Gentile.

The church acts on God's behalf when it judges.

In verse 18 Jesus tells us why God has given the church such authority. It's for the reason we have already talked about: The church is to act as God's earthly court, rendering His heavenly decisions on earth.

In fact, Jesus goes on to give this promise, which is often used as a general promise of answered prayer: "If two of you agree on earth about anything that they may ask, it shall be done for them by My Father who is in heaven. For where two or three have gathered together in My name, there I am in their midst" (vv. 19–20).

Gathered for what? For prayer? To hear the Word of God? Is that what Jesus is talking about? Well, we need to gather together for both of those things; however, that is not is what Jesus has in mind here. He's saying that when the church gathers together to render its judgments and decisions, He will be in the midst of His people. Now that process will certainly include the use of prayer and the Word, but for the specific purpose of judging.

So, since the church acts on God's behalf when it judges, this is the court a believer should go to if he or she wants to be blessed. As we saw above, Paul says that, if we have to go to the secular courts to settle issues in the church, we have already lost.

That is where the rubber of our Christianity meets the road of real life. Being a Christian is more than just singing and praising God. We are also to render His judgments because the church is a family court, if you will.

And just as you wouldn't want your children taking the family business out into the street, God does not want you and me taking kingdom business out into the street, to people who don't have a kingdom mentality.

Here is why some people don't want to come to the church with their marital disputes. They don't want to subject themselves to the rule of God, because His goal is always to preserve the marriage covenant. People want to go to somebody who is going to say, "Do whatever you want."

Our kids are like that. If they can't get what they want from one parent, they go the other. They don't want to be handed a righteous decision. They only want to hear *their* decision. But God says we can't do that as His people. We are to render His judgments, and we have His promise that He will be right there with us in the middle of the process if we will follow His instructions.

SUMMING IT UP

So, how does all of this relate to marriage and divorce? Look at 1 Corinthians 7:39: "A wife is bound as long as her husband lives; but if her husband is dead, she is free to be married to whom she wishes, only in the Lord."

This is as good a summary statement of the issue as you will find. Everything I have outlined can be summarized right here. As long as a person's marriage partner is alive, either physically or covenantally (spiritually), then he or she is bound to that mate. The most that can be done is to separate and remain unmarried or be reconciled (we saw that in 7:10). There are no grounds for a divorce that leads to remarriage as long as the partner is alive.

If a person is dead spiritually because of unrepentant sin, he or she must be declared dead by God's coroner, the church. Once that person is declared dead, he is to be treated as a Gentile and a tax collector or delivered to the realm of Satan (1 Corinthians 5:5), and the partner is free to remarry.

Why? Because God has revoked the previous marriage covenant. May I say it once more? God hates divorce. He never commands it. He only permits it when death occurs in order to preserve and protect the innocent party. Biblical justice demands that the rights and well-being of the victim be protected. So there are three options for the Christian whose marriage partner has been declared covenantally or spiritually dead.

The first option is to forgive and restore the partner to the relationship based on repentance and restitution (Exodus 21:28–31; Leviticus 6:1–7; Matthew 18:33–35). Of course, this should always be the first option, to see if we can fix what got broken.

A major question that arises regarding the issue of restitution is whether this demands that an adulterous mate should always confess the sin to his or her mate. While each situation must be evaluated individually, my normal answer is yes, unless some extenuating emotional, physical, or spiritual circumstance demands otherwise. This is so because intercourse establishes an illegitimate covenant that needs to be nullified. Also, intercourse opens up the potential of the transfer of disease to the innocent party. There's an old saying, however, that "you can't mold dry clay." Thus it is crucial that the proper preparation be made of moistening the relationship with your spouse before confession is made. A person in this situation should seek the counsel of a godly friend or pastor to help walk with him or her through this process of confession and restitution.

If your mate does something that produces covenant death, but is sincerely repentant, forgiveness is always possible. The man in 1 Corinthians 5 repented, and Paul told the church to restore him (2 Corinthians 2:6–7).

How do you know when someone is sincerely repentant? It takes a lot more than words, because none of us can know another person's heart. That's why the Bible says people who are repentant must demonstrate it by bringing forth the fruit of repentance (Matthew 3:8; Ephesians 5:8–9).

There must be a change of heart and an attempt to repay the offended party for what was lost. In the case of marriage, the sinning partner needs to demonstrate by his or her actions repentance and determination to be faithful to the marriage covenant. This is the fruit of repentance.

By the way, this is the only reason God accepted the marriage of David to Bathsheba. He took restitution out on David because David had said in response to Nathan the prophet's story, "May the man who did this thing pay it back fourfold" (see 2 Samuel 12:1–6). So David lost four of his sons after he committed the sin of adultery and killed Bathsheba's husband. Instead of killing David, God took restitution.

If you have offended your mate, you need to make restitution. That could involve any number of things based on the infraction. One man wrote out a covenant to his wife, spelling out the ways he would check himself and remain faithful to her from the point of her forgiveness on, and he made it so that she could hold him accountable. This can be determined with the help of a good Christian counselor, which is always a good place to start.

The second option for a Christian is to divorce the covenantally dead spouse. This option permits remarriage (Deuteronomy 24:1; Matthew 5:31–32; Romans 7:1–3).

This is the path Joseph was going to take with Mary (Matthew 1:19) when he thought she had committed immorality. He had decided to "put her away secretly," which meant divorce her, before God intervened and revealed the truth to him. Sometimes this option involves the right of the victim to forgive the sin without necessarily alleviating the consequences (2 Samuel 12:13–14). This option, however, must not be taken without receiving approval (bill of divorcement) from the church.

The third option is to live with a covenantally dead spouse even though that person may be unrepentant about his or her sin (1 Corinthians 7:12–13). This is the scenario for the unbeliever or spiritually dead person who wants to stay in the marriage.

If he or she is willing to function as a husband or wife, Paul says the believer should not leave or put the unbeliever out. In this case, your marriage becomes an opportunity for evangelism and the believing mate has a sanctifying effect on the family.

Now, Paul is not talking about a wife staying in a marriage where her husband is beating her every day or abandoning his responsibilities, as we talked about earlier. He is talking about an unbelieving mate who is willing to function properly in his role within the marriage covenant. If you have a non-Christian spouse, you can stay and pray and trust God to work through you to bring about a change.

There are legions of believers, mostly women, who are faithful and loving spouses to non-Christians because they take their wedding vows seriously. They will be first in the kingdom.

Those are the three options: restoration based on repentance and restitution; divorce based on death, which always allows for remarriage; and staying with the unbelieving or excommunicated mate so that God can use you to bring that person to Himself.

Before we conclude, let me add an important parenthetical word to those who were divorced before they became Christians. If you were divorced before you were saved and you are still single, you are free to remarry in the Lord since salvation offers you a brand-new beginning (2 Corinthians 5:17).

A FINAL WORD OF HOPE

Some of us have messed up for five years. Others of us have messed up for ten years. Still others have messed up for twenty years. Most of us have just plain messed up.

But, when Jesus hung on the cross, He said, "It is finished," which meant He had paid our sin debt in full. When He rose from the dead on the third day, the receipt verifying His payment was written and issued to us.

That's good news because it means that no matter how hopeless your marriage is, there is hope. No matter how bleak your circumstances, there is hope. No matter how badly you or your mate has blown it, there is hope, because Jesus paid it all. The debt of your sin and mine has been covered.

If you are a Christian, every day you get up you ought to thank God for Jesus, because He ever lives to make intercession for you. This new relationship is called the new covenant, founded on the blood of Christ. Because Christ died in our place and for our sin, God has made a new arrangement with us.

So in Christ there is hope for you individually and for your marriage. Even if your marriage is a shambles, even if you got married or remarried out of the will of God, I am here to give you good news. You can't make a mess bad enough that Jesus isn't powerful enough to fix.

The message of the new covenant is that He meets us in our sin and offers us a brand-new start every day. Every day, we have a new opportunity to renew our covenant with God and begin a new walk with Him. I don't know anybody else offering that kind of deal around town these days.

As I said, this is not only true for your personal life, it is true for your relationships. In 1 Corinthians 11:17–34 we have a picture of a church that had floundered in every conceivable area. There was moral failure. There were legal failures. There were people committing the sin of alcoholism. They were even coming to church drunk. How bad can you get?

But in the midst of this mess, Paul reminds the Corinthians and us that we live under a new covenant that not only gets us right with God but can get us right with each other. It can restore and restart relationships —and that includes your marriage.

The new covenant can take a marriage on the skids and turn it completely around. It can take an illegitimate marriage and legitimize it. Paul is saying that, when you hold the body and blood of Christ in your hands, you are holding a brand-new beginning. There is forgiveness of sin.

So every time you come to the new covenant, you come asking for a fresh start. You come asking for another chance. I'm sure glad God does not run out of new chances. Many of us have given our marriage partners their last chance. "You did it to me once. You did it to me twice. I'm not going to give you a chance to do it to me again."

God says that when we hold up His Son Jesus, He can't help but give us another chance. Not because He feels good about us, but because He feels good about His Son. His Son paid our sin debt in full, and we have the receipt of the resurrection to prove it.

See, the world can't give you that. If you have messed up in your marriage, all the world can do is give you a lot of dead-end options. Throw in the towel. Get rid of your mate. Try it again. Enjoy sex without being tied down by a piece of paper.

But there is another option. It comes in a person. It comes with nail prints in the hands and a wound in the side and a body drained of blood. The risen Jesus Christ has made restitution to God for your sin. And He can give you the power to forgive and to restore your marriage, if you will come to Him in faith and trust Him to do the work.

The good news is that in the gospel there is hope. This is why Jesus could say to a woman caught in adultery, "From now on sin no more" (John 8:11). Even though she deserved to die, even though judgment was sure, Jesus covered her with His blood. His death and resurrection were her receipt.

What does that mean? Where do you go with that? It means you can begin the rest of your life today. No matter what divorces you have gone through or remarriages you have entered into, today you can begin the rest of your life.

Nobody can offer you that but God. You say, "But, Tony, you don't know what I did!" No, you don't know what Christ did.

You say, "Well, I made a mess." That's why God made a miracle.

You say, "But I messed up." That's why Jesus got up from the grave. He got up because you messed up.

You say, "But I am so discouraged." But Jesus is alive! And as long as you are alive, there is hope for your marriage. Even if you have failed in the past, you can start from where you are and sin no more. Today is a day of hope.

You say, "I can't fix the mess I made yesterday." But Jesus can. If your marriage is in turmoil or you have already remarried out of God's will, but you are willing to repent for what you have done, then you and your partner can enter into a new covenant and find the same grace that David and Bathsheba found when God recognized their new relationship even though it was born out of adultery (2 Samuel 12:24–25).

Let me hasten to warn you, however, that God's grace is not to be trifled with. You can't keep repeating the same sin over and over and not expect to receive God's fiery judgment (Hebrews 10:26–27).

My friend, God does not change His standards. His will for you and me in marriage is a one-flesh relationship for life. However, we often fail to meet His standards; we fall short of His glory (Romans 3:23). But the good news of the gospel is that Christ has issued a receipt to cover us when we fail and to give us a brand-new start. So begin today, and "go and sin no more."

THE URBAN ALTERNATIVE

The Philosophy

Dr. Tony Evans and TUA believe the answer to transforming our culture comes from the inside out and from the bottom up. We believe the core cause of the problems we face is a spiritual one; therefore, the only way to address them is spiritually. And that means the proclamation and application of biblical principles to the four areas of life—the individual, the family, the church, and the community. We've tried a political, social, economic, and even a religious agenda. It's time for a kingdom agenda.

The Purpose

We believe that when each biblical sphere of life functions properly, the net result is evangelism, discipleship, and community impact. As people learn how to govern themselves under God, they then transform the institutions of family, church, and government from a biblically based kingdom perspective.

The Programs

To achieve our goal we use a variety of strategies, methods, and resources for reaching and equipping as many people as possible.

- Broadcast Media
  The Urban Alternative reaches hundreds of thousands of people each day with a kingdom-based approach to life through its daily radio program, weekly television broadcast, and the Internet.

- Leadership Training
  Our national Church Development Conference, held annually, equips pastors and lay leaders to become agents of change. Teaching biblical methods of church ministry has helped congregations renew their sense of mission and expand their ministry impact.

- Crusades/Conferences
  Crusades are designed to bring churches together across racial, cultural, and denominational lines to win the lost. TUA also seeks to keep these churches together for ongoing fellowship and community impact. Conferences give Christians practical biblical insight on how to live victoriously in accordance with God's Word and His kingdom agenda in the four areas of life—personal, family, church, and community.

- Resource Development
  We are fostering lifelong learning partnerships with the people we serve by providing a variety of published materials. We offer books, audiotapes,

videos, and booklets to strengthen people in their walk with God and ministry to others.

- **Project Turn-Around**
PTA is a comprehensive church-based community impact strategy. It addresses such areas as economic development, education, housing, health revitalization, family renewal and reconciliation. To model the success of the project, TUA invests in its own program locally. We also assist other churches in tailoring the model to meet the specific needs of their communities, while simultaneously addressing the spiritual and moral frame of reference.

* * *

For more information, a catalog of Dr. Tony Evans's ministry resources, and a complimentary copy of Dr. Evans's monthly devotional magazine,
call (800) 800-3222 or
write TUA at P.O. Box 4000, Dallas TX 75208.